DECADES OF THE 20th AND 21st CENTURIES

# The 1940s

Stephen Feinstein

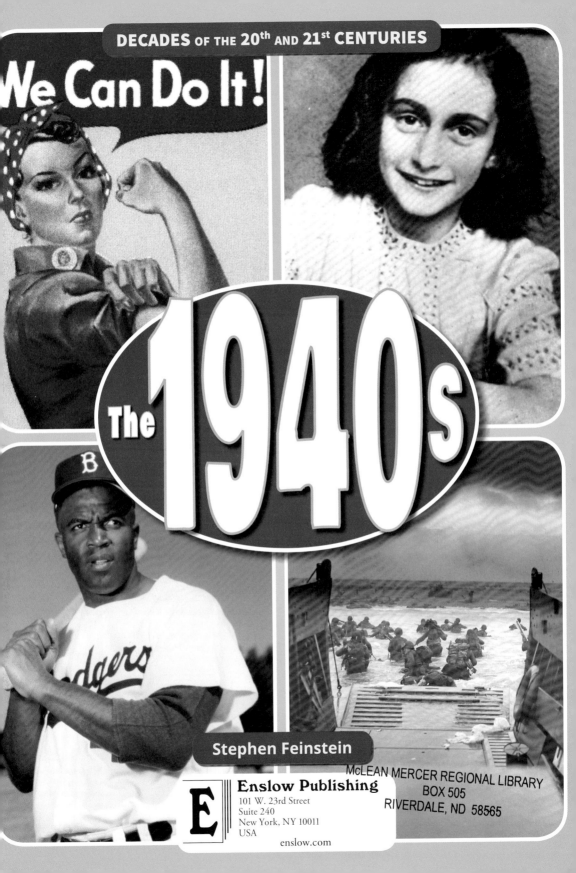

We Can Do It!

# The 1940s

Stephen Feinstein

**E** **Enslow Publishing**
101 W. 23rd Street
Suite 240
New York, NY 10011
USA
enslow.com

Published in 2016 by Enslow Publishing, LLC.
101 W. 23rd Street, Suite 240, New York, NY 10011

**Library of Congress Cataloging-in-Publication Data**

Feinstein, Stephen.
 The 1940s / Stephen Feinstein.
   pages cm. — (Decades of the 20th and 21st centuries)
 Includes bibliographical references and index.
 Summary: "Discusses the decade 1940-1949 in the United States in terms of culture, art, science, and poli-
tics"—Provided by publisher.
 Audience: Grade 9 to 12.
 ISBN 978-0-7660-6928-2
 1. United States—Civilization—1918-1945—Juvenile literature. 2. United States—Civilization—1945- —Ju-
venile literature. 3. United States—Politics and government—1933-1945—Juvenile literature.
 4. United States—Politics and government—1945-1953—Juvenile literature. 5. Nineteen forties—
Juvenile literature. I. Title.
 E169.1.F356 2015
 973.918—dc23

                              2015010946

Printed in the United States of America

**To Our Readers:** We have done our best to make sure all Web sites in this book were active and appropriate when we went to press. However, the author and the publisher have no control over and assume no liability for the material available on those Web sites or on any Web sites they may link to. Any comments or sugges-tions can be sent by e-mail to customerservice@enslow.com.

**Photo Credits:** AFP/Getty Images, p. 75; Alfred Eisenstaedt/The LIFE Picture Collection/Getty Images, p. 85; Arthur Brower/New York Times Co./Getty Images, pp. 55, 87 (bottom); Authenticated News/Archive Photos/Getty Images, p. 16; Central Press/Getty Images, p. 73; CPHoM Robert F. Sargent/National Archives and Records/Into the Jaws of Death/public domain, p. 3 (bottom right); Dorothea Lange/Interim Archives/ Getty Images, p. 52; Everett Historical/Shutterstock.com, p. 6; Fotosearch/Getty Images, p. 56; Gates/Hulton Archive/Getty Images, p. 14; George Skadding/The LIFE Picture Collection/Getty Images), pp. 62, 88 (bot-tom); Georgi Zelma/Slava Katamidze Collection/Getty Images, p. 59; Gjon Mili/The LIFE Picture Collection/ Getty Images, p. 34;  Harold M. Lambert/Lambert/Getty Images, p. 13; Hulton Archive/Archive Photos/Getty Images, p. 24; Hulton Archive/Getty Images, pp. 23, 66; Hugo Jaeger/The LIFE Picture Collection/Getty Images, pp. 45, 87 (top); Jewish Chronicle/Heritage Images/Getty Images, pp. 3 (top right), 32; Keystone-France/Gamma-Keystone via Getty Images, pp. 69, 82; Keystone/Getty Images, pp. 42, 47, 89 (bottom); Keystone View/FPG/Hulton Archive, Getty Images, p. 18; Metronome/Archive Photos/Getty Images, p. 37; Mondadori Portfolio via Getty Images, p. 29; NBC Television/Getty Images, p. 21; Photo File/MLB Photos via Getty Images, pp. 3 (bottom left), 38, 90; Photo Reproduction by Transcendental Graphics/Getty Images, p. 41; Popperfoto/Getty Images, pp. 74, 79; Portfolio via Getty Images, p. 77; RKO Radio Pictures/Getty Im-ages, p. 31; Roger Viollet/Getty Images, p. 60; The National Archives/SSPL/Getty Images, p. 10; TinaImages/ Shutterstock.com, p. 3 (top left); Universal History Archive/Getty Images, pp. 48, 51, 65; Vintage Images/ Getty Images, pp. 80, 89 (top); Warner Brothers/Getty Images, pp. 26, 88 (top); Yevgeny Khaldei/Getty Im-ages, p. 70.

**Cover Credits:** CPHoM Robert F. Sargent/National Archives and Records/Into the Jaws of Death/public domain (D-Day); Jewish Chronicle/Heritage Images/Getty Images (Anne Frank); Photo File/MLB Photos via Getty Images (Jackie Robinson); TinaImages/Shutterstock.com (Rosie the Riveter).

# Contents

*The attack on Pearl Harbor brought America into World War II.*

# Introduction

The 1930s were difficult years for most Americans. Millions had to endure extreme poverty and hunger during the Great Depression, an economic collapse that affected the whole world. Under President Franklin D. Roosevelt, the nation pulled out of the depths of the Depression. But the economy was still weak, and many Americans remained unemployed.

As the 1940s began, Americans hoped for an improvement in their lives—better job opportunities and financial security. Although much of the world was at war, Americans were more concerned with domestic matters. In fact, most thought isolationism—avoiding involvement in conflicts abroad—was the best policy for America. As bad as things seemed overseas, the problems there did not seem to concern America. When Roosevelt ran for an unprecedented third term as president in 1940, he told Americans that he would not send their sons to fight overseas. This was what Americans wanted to hear. They voted Roosevelt into office again.

On December 7, 1941, Japan carried out a surprise air attack on the US naval base at Pearl Harbor, Hawaii. By December 11, the United States was at war. By its end in 1945, the war would change the United States, its economy, and the decade of the 1940s in dramatic ways. By far, World War II was the biggest event of the decade and the worst conflict in human history. Roughly sixty million people died in the war. At least half of the war's victims were civilians. Some were bystanders killed in by bombs and shelling. Others were victims of disease and starvation. Still others were executed because of their race or religion.

World War II officially began on September 1, 1939, when Nazi Germany invaded Poland. Germany had fallen into a dire economic crisis. Its citizens were unemployed and starving. Many Germans fell under the spell of charismatic leader Adolf Hitler. Hitler built his Nazi Party using fear and hate, but he also promised full recovery of Germany. The German people became fully devoted to him. Hitler's plan for economic recovery had Germans building tanks, airplanes, and submarines to create a strong military. Soon, Hitler was using it to threaten nearby nations.

A similar problem was developing in Japan. The military ran the nation and demanded absolute loyalty from the Japanese people. Before long, Japan was also threatening its neighbors with its war weapons. In 1937, it launched a full-scale invasion of China. Japanese troops also seized other land in Asia and the Pacific Ocean. These acts created fierce tension between Japan and the United States.

By the end of 1941, every major nation in the world was at war. Germany, Japan, and Italy banded together to form the Axis powers. Those who opposed them were known as the Allies, led by Great Britain, the Soviet Union, and the United States. Before the war ended in 1945, more than sixty countries had taken part.

World War II changed America in many ways. With millions of men overseas, women made up a larger part of the workforce. About three million women took factory jobs. They showed that they could do the same work as men. African Americans also stepped forward. They fought bravely even though their country treated them as second-class citizens. When the war was over, many women and African Americans were unwilling to return to a lesser position in American society. World War II caused many other important changes. It affected American business, sports, and the arts.

# Pop Culture, Lifestyles, and Fashion

Americans were used to buying whatever they wanted whenever they wanted—if they had enough money to make the purchase. Once the United States entered World War II, people were suddenly faced with restrictions on what and how much they could buy.

## Patriotism and Rationing

On December 27, 1941, the government announced a rationing of rubber tires. A rubber shortage had come about almost overnight. There was a shortage of gasoline during the war, as well. The military needed it for jeeps, tanks, planes, and ships. As a result, there was little gas left over for civilians to put in their cars. The government gave out ration coupons. These coupons enabled each family to buy a small amount of gas each week. Rationing ensured that everyone received a fair share.

Soon the new federal Office of Price Administration (OPA) announced that various other goods would also be strictly rationed, including sugar, coffee, meat, fats and oils, cheese, and shoes. The OPA also issued books of ration stamps, which had to be used to buy rationed goods. Americans had no choice but to go along with the OPA's rationing system. Surprisingly, Americans ate better during the

**DIG ON FOR VICTORY**

Americans grew victory gardens to help the nation's food supply.

war years than they did during the 1930s. Even though many food products were strictly rationed, the need for factories to produce huge amounts of goods for fighting the war meant that most people had jobs. They could afford to buy more of whatever was available.

Another factor contributed to the nation's food supply during the war. The government encouraged Americans to plant vegetables in their backyards. That way, commercial farmers could feed the army rather than ordinary customers. Inspired by feelings of patriotism and a sense of practicality, many Americans enthusiastically grew victory gardens, as their backyard minifarms were called. In 1943, victory gardens produced about one third of all the vegetables consumed in the United States.

America's children also played an important role in the nation's wartime efforts. They participated in drives to collect scrap metals, rubber, tin cans, and other waste products that were recycled into wartime production. Under the War Finance Program, children in school bought more than $100 million worth of War Stamps with their nickels and dimes. They then traded in filled books of stamps for War Bonds. The sales of War Bonds paid for more than 44,000 jeeps, 2,900 planes, and 11,700 parachutes in 1944 alone.

## Women Keep the War Machine Running

During the war years, the number of American women who worked increased from about 12 million to about 18.5 million. Inspired by Lockheed Aircraft's mythical Rosie the Riveter, whose picture appeared on posters all around the country, many women put on coveralls and followed Rosie to jobs at defense-related factories.

Women soon proved they could do just as well as men at performing many of the industrial assembly-line jobs that had been previously held only by men. Before the war, about twelve million American women were working outside the home. They made up around one quarter of the US workforce in such positions as maids, secretaries, teachers, and nurses. By the end of the war, however, women made up about 36 percent of the civilian workforce. With millions of men serving in the military, factories started to hire female workers. Women filled a wide variety of jobs. Some women welded airplane parts together. Some operated cranes in shipyards. For most, it was their first experience with factory employment. They learned their jobs well and worked long hours. With their help, wartime production had proceeded at an astounding pace.

The sheer volume of American production was overwhelming. It helped bring the United States and its allies victory in the war. In just five years, 1940 to 1945, US factories produced almost 300,000 aircraft, 71,000 naval ships, 5,000 cargo ships, about 300,000 artillery pieces, 20 million small arms, 41.5 billion rounds of small arms ammunition, almost 6 million aircraft bombs, more than 100,000 tanks and self-propelled guns, and about 2.5 million army trucks.

## Women in the Military

Not only were American women working at factory jobs, but for the first time, some women enlisted in the military. Some served in the new Women's Army Auxiliary Corps (WACs). Others joined a branch of the navy called Women Accepted for Volunteer Emergency Service (WAVES). And some women served as fliers in the Women's Auxiliary Ferrying Squadron (WAFS). Women were not assigned to combat duty. Instead, they did jobs that allowed more men to be available for combat. By 1945, more than two hundred thousand women were actively serving in the armed forces.

## War's Effect on Fashion

Because much of the nation's clothing industry during the war was working to provide uniforms for the military, there was far less fabric

Women took over factory jobs when American men went off to war.

U.S.A. 4300703

Women contributed to the war effort by joining the military.

for other kinds of clothing. The government set strict guidelines on the amount of fabric to be used in various items of clothing. Fabric shortages encouraged a trend toward simpler styles, such as wrap-around skirts.

Long evening dresses were replaced with shorter ones. Short sleeves replaced long sleeves. Coats had no cuffs, and blouses had no pockets or ruffles. Because there were also restrictions on the use of metal for zippers and other fasteners, designers created a dress that draped so it needed only two buttons. Women who worked in factories wore the same type of clothing on the job as their male coworkers. Work outfits were sturdy coveralls or jumpsuits, hard hats, tool belts, and thick-soled shoes. Away from the job, women preferred clothing that showed their femininity, such as belted or tailored dresses that were pinched in the waist.

After the war, women's fashion took off in a completely different direction. No longer were fabrics in short supply. Paris, which had been occupied by Germany during the war, was once again the center of fashion. Parisian fashion designer Christian Dior introduced his new look, which emphasized a woman's curves. His designs featured a tiny waistline; long, full skirts; sloping shoulders; and soft, full collars and sleeves.

## Nylon Replaces Silk

In 1940, Du Pont introduced a new synthetic fiber called nylon. It was said to be as strong as elastic, but it had the sheerness of silk. The company planned to use nylon to replace the traditional silk stocking.

Once America entered the war, silk stockings became unavailable because Japan, one of the nations that the United States was fighting, stopped exporting silk. As a result, the US government ordered that nylon be used to make parachutes, tents, and other war supplies—not women's stockings. During the war, some women drew fake seams on

# The Bikini

In 1946, a new type of swimwear, called a bikini, was introduced. It was named after Bikini Atoll, a small island in the western Pacific Ocean. On Bikini, the United States had tested nuclear bombs. For most Americans, who were used to one-piece bathing suits, the sight of a woman on the beach in a skimpy two-piece bathing suit was quite startling. It would take years for the novelty to wear off and for the racy new swimsuit to become a common sight.

their legs with an eyebrow pencil to make it look as though they were wearing stockings even though they were not.

## The Controversy over Zoot Suits

Young men, mainly African Americans and poor whites, began wearing a new type of outfit in the early 1940s that defied conventional styles. Known as a zoot suit, the style featured baggy pants that tapered from sixteen inches wide at the knee to six inches at the pegged bottom. With the pants was a jacket with overstuffed shoulders that reached down to the knees and was usually worn unbuttoned. A key chain that almost dragged on the floor was often worn.

The baggy zoot suit fad also became very popular with young Mexican Americans, known as Pachucos, in Los Angeles, California. Unfortunately, the zoot suit played a key role in a shameful episode of racist violence. In June 1943 in Los Angeles, a mob of about twenty-five hundred white sailors and soldiers attacked about one hundred Mexican Americans wearing zoot suits. Supposedly, there had been a rumor that a gang of Pachucos had beaten up a sailor. In response, the servicemen began beating up anyone they saw wearing a zoot suit. After the military police put an end to the riot, the Los Angeles City Council outlawed the wearing of zoot suits.

## America Expands

In the early 1940s, the birthrate began to rise dramatically. Many young couples rushed to get married and have children before the husband could be sent off to war. By 1943, the birthrate had risen to a sixteen-year peak.

But it was not until after the war in 1946 that the true baby boom, which would last for the next eighteen years, began. The war was over. The husbands were back. And young men and women who were still single rushed to get married. It was a perfect time to start a family. Jobs were plentiful, rationing had ended, and America appeared prosperous. In 1946, the birthrate had increased by nearly 20 percent from the previous year. Seventy-four percent of couples had their first child during their first year of marriage.

## A Growing Middle Class

The major social and cultural trends that would characterize the 1950s began during the years immediately following the end of World War II. While the majority of Americans before the war were poor, most Americans after the war had money to spend. A new law, the

### Dr. Spock

In 1946, Dr. Benjamin Spock published his book *Common Sense Book of Baby and Child Care*, which led to a revolution in the way children were raised. Dr. Spock believed that parents should not subject their children to harsh discipline because there was no such thing as a bad child even if a child's behavior was bad. Spock advised parents to listen to their children, respond to them, and respect their wishes when appropriate. People who believed that the traditional strict discipline of children was necessary accused Spock of being too permissive. Nevertheless, millions of American parents read Spock's book and followed his suggestions.

Servicemen's Readjustment Act, known as the G.I. Bill of Rights, was signed by President Roosevelt on June 22, 1944. As a result, millions of veterans returning from the war were provided with low-interest housing loans and generous college scholarships. A vast new middle class of consumers bought new cars, new homes in new suburban subdivisions, and all kinds of household appliances, including a revolutionary new appliance called a television.

A rising middle class had money to spend on radios and televisions.

# Entertainment and the Arts

The arts and entertainment in America during wartime could not avoid being influenced by World War II. With everyone's mind on war, movies, books, and music of the day reflected the struggles overseas and at home. But in the years following the horrors of the war, art took a daring turn into dark realism.

## The War's Influence

Popular songs of the times included tunes such as "Let's Knock the Hit out of Hitler," "He's 1-A in the Army and He's A-1 in My Heart," and "The Boogie Woogie Bugle Boy of Company B."

Popular comic strip heroes, such as Ham Fisher's boxer Joe Palooka, joined the army for the duration of the war. Curiously, Superman was ruled 4-F, or ineligible for service, by his local draft board because of his X-ray vision! Instead of fighting America's enemies, the man of steel had to spend the war years raising money for the Red Cross. Meanwhile, Little Orphan Annie went around urging kids to collect scrap metal for the war effort. Likewise, illustrator Norman Rockwell created a series of *Saturday Evening Post* covers featuring Willie Gillis, a young man who goes off to war and finally returns home safely. One of Rockwell's covers also featured Rosie the Riveter.

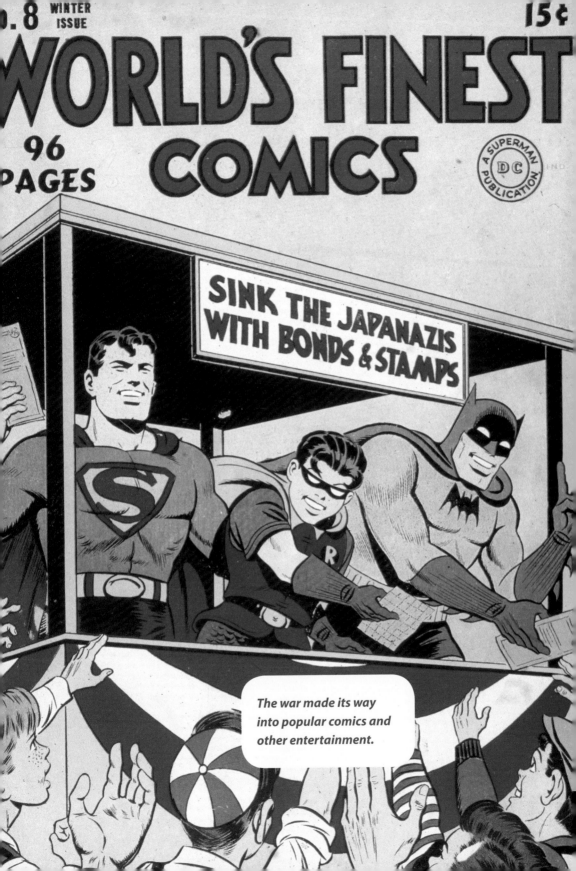

The war made its way into popular comics and other entertainment.

# Entertaining the Troops

In 1941, a new group was created to entertain resting soldiers. Called the United Service Organizations, or USO, it opened clubs around the world for American soldiers. Each club tried to make the soldiers feel as if they were at home.

There were dances, movies, and games. The USO also hosted live shows by Hollywood stars. Famous performers, such as Humphrey Bogart, Bette Davis, and Frank Sinatra, entertained the troops. By 1944, the USO was hosting seven hundred shows per day around the globe.

Bob Hope (*above*) was a famous comedian who spent much of his career entertaining American soldiers. For fifty years, troops from four different wars laughed at his jokes. In 1997, President Bill Clinton named Hope an honorary veteran for his dedication to the US military. Bob Hope died six years later at the age of one hundred.

# Movies During the War

Movies probably did the most to evoke feelings of patriotism and raise people's spirits. Hollywood cranked out an endless stream of war-related movies throughout the war years. Even during the period before America's entry into the war, Hollywood had begun to release films with an anti-Nazi message. Nazis were the Germans under Adolf Hitler against whom the Allies were fighting in Europe. Among these films were *Confessions of a Nazi Spy* (1939), Charlie Chaplin's spoof of Hitler *The Great Dictator* (1940), and *I Married a Nazi* (1940).

Within six months of the bombing of Pearl Harbor, seventy war-related movies were released in theaters. Many were about real events, such as *Remember Pearl Harbor*. Because of America's anger toward Japan, these films often used terrible racist stereotyping and depicted the Japanese as evil, bucktoothed, subhuman caricatures.

Other films were about typical Hollywood heroes, such as Tarzan, who now had to fight Nazis in the African jungle. There were also gangster movies in which the bad guys became Nazi spies. Various other Hollywood movies portrayed the contributions and sacrifices of Americans who played important roles in the war effort. Possibly the biggest hit film of the World War II years was *Casablanca* (1942), starring Humphrey Bogart and Ingrid Bergman.

In addition to popular films, directors such as Frank Capra produced a series of documentaries called *Why We Fight*. They explained how the United States had become involved in the war. Even Walt Disney created films in support of the war effort, such as *Victory Through Airpower*.

To make sure that Hollywood filmmakers were giving the appropriate message, in June 1942, President Roosevelt created the Office of War Information (OWI), a government propaganda agency. The OWI set up an office in Hollywood. Studios were asked to submit film scripts before shooting began. The OWI reviewed scripts and suggested

Casablanca *is considered one of the greatest love stories, even today.*

changes, if necessary, so the film would present the government's view of the country and the war.

## Hollywood's Red Scare

Under the supervision and enthusiastic support of the OWI, Hollywood produced a number of propaganda films, including *The North Star* (1943), which portrayed America's Soviet allies in a sympathetic light. *The North Star's* screenplay was written by Lillian Hellman, its musical score was by Aaron Copland, and its lyrics were by Ira Gershwin.

But in the years after the war, the political landscape of the world changed radically. The Soviet Union, America's wartime ally, had become the United States' enemy. After World War II ended, the victorious Allies divided Europe among themselves to ensure that the war-torn countries would be rebuilt and governed properly. The communist Soviet Union took over the governments of several Eastern European nations and made them part of the communist system. The United States feared communism and believed its goal was to take over the whole world and eliminate democratic systems, such as America's. Therefore, many American leaders worked hard to prevent Soviet influence from spreading. During the long period known as the Cold War, the United States and the Soviet Union opposed each other fiercely while building weapons and trying to gain influence with other nations around the world. However, the two nations never fought an actual battle.

Cold War tensions carried over into many aspects of American life. Although President Harry Truman disbanded the OWI in 1945, Hollywood's brief period of freedom from government interference came to an end in 1947. That year, the newly established House Committee on Un-American Activities (HUAC) began investigating Hollywood. Committee members looked for communists working in the film industry—people guilty of producing pro-Soviet films, such as *Song of Russia* and *The North Star*.

In October 1947, HUAC held hearings in Washington, D.C. Among those summoned to testify were ten Hollywood screenwriters. A group of Hollywood celebrities, including Humphrey Bogart, Lauren Bacall, John Huston, and Danny Kaye, traveled to Washington to protest the hearings. The Hollywood Ten, as the screenwriters were called, refused to cooperate with the committee. They were fined and jailed. They were among hundreds who would be blacklisted. The blacklist held names of people that the makers of the list considered dangerous or unacceptable. No studio would hire them for many years to come.

## Film Noir

After the war ended, a new type of suspense film, known as film noir, became popular in the United States. Movies of this genre, filmed in stark black and white and featuring odd camera angles, usually had a bleak urban setting. Their stories were often based on detective novels. The hero typically had to deal with personal obsessions, dangerous delusions, and romantic or other goals that were difficult or impossible to achieve. It seems strange that a dark, moody type of film could have struck a chord with American moviegoers in a time of optimism and prosperity. Perhaps the growing sense of insecurity that came with the onset of the Cold War had something to do with it. Or perhaps the horrors of World War II had given Americans a cynical awareness and appreciation of the dark side of human nature.

The first film noir was director John Huston's *The Maltese Falcon*, starring Humphrey Bogart. Produced in 1941, it would influence the film noir movies made after the war.

Humphrey Bogart starred in the film classic The Maltese Falcon.

## Citizen Kane

Orson Welles's *Citizen Kane* (1943) is often considered the greatest film ever made. Yet very few people in the 1940s ever had the opportunity to see it.

Welles created a devastating fictional portrayal of the life of powerful newspaper publisher William Randolph Hearst. RKO Studios had allowed twenty-five-year-old Welles to produce the film without any supervision or interference from studio executives. When Hearst learned about the film, however, he tried to prevent its release by threatening legal action against RKO. As a result, there was only a limited release of *Citizen Kane*. Still, critics loved it, and the movie won nine Academy Award nominations and one Oscar for best screenplay.

# Combat Novels and American Modernism

Many American novelists during the 1940s also focused on the war. Thus a new type of fiction was born, known as the combat novel. The best of this genre included works such as Norman Mailer's *The Naked and the Dead* (1948), which described the terror of combat and the boredom of army life.

Writers in the 1940s focused on the individual and his or her place in the modern world. Representing this new style of modernism in American writing were novelists, such as Saul Bellow, Truman Capote, Paul Bowles, and John Hawkes. African American writer Richard Wright was also popular. He dealt with the oppression of blacks, but his work was closer in spirit to the socialist realist writers of the 1930s. His novel *Native Son* (1940) and autobiography, *Black Boy* (1945), were widely read by white Americans as well as blacks.

# Tennessee Williams and Arthur Miller

The two most successful American playwrights of the 1940s were Tennessee Williams and Arthur Miller. Both men tried to depict life

Welles's Charles Foster Kane is one of cinema's greatest characters.

# Anne Frank

World War II touched nearly everyone's life in some way. Many people wrote about their experiences during the war. One of the most compelling and enduring stories came from a young Jewish girl named Anne Frank, who lived in Amsterdam during the Nazi occupation.

The Frank family was forced to hide inside secret rooms in an office building. If found, they would be sent to a concentration camp. For her thirteenth birthday, Anne received a diary. She wrote about her hopes, dreams, and fears. After two years, the Nazis discovered Anne and her family. Most of the Frank family, including Anne, died in a concentration camp. Two years after the war ended, her diary was published. Anne's story gave a face to the tragedy of the Holocaust.

in America realistically. Thomas Lanier Williams, who became known as Tennessee Williams, focused on the frustrations, illusions, and emotional conflicts of ordinary people in his plays *The Glass Menagerie* (1945), *A Streetcar Named Desire* (1947), and *Summer and Smoke* (1948). Arthur Miller, in his plays *All My Sons* (1947) and *Death of a Salesman* (1949), dealt with the conflict between fathers and sons.

## Escape Through Broadway Musicals

Throughout the 1940s, the Broadway musical proved to be popular with many Americans. Audiences probably enjoyed a couple of hours of escape from the world's troubles just as much as they appreciated the musicals' spectacular dancing and memorable tunes. Especially successful were Rodgers and Hammerstein's *Oklahoma!* (1943) and *Carousel* (1945), Irving Berlin's *Annie Get Your Gun* (1946), and Cole Porter's *Kiss Me, Kate* (1948).

## The Rise of Television

A major innovation that would have an effect on the lifestyles of Americans, and people all over the world, had been in development for years. On July 1, 1941, the CBS and NBC television networks began broadcasting fifteen hours of programming a week. But television sets were expensive. By late 1941, only about fifteen thousand televisions were in use. Once the United States entered World War II, further development of television was put on hold. After the war, television production and broadcasting resumed. Television sets soon became much more affordable.

The most popular show in the late 1940s was *Texaco Star Theater*. It was a variety show starring comedian Milton Berle. By the fall of 1948, 94.7 percent of television viewers in the United States were watching the program. Berle became known as Mr. Television. Many television viewers affectionately referred to him as Uncle Miltie.

Dancing the jitterbug to the music of big bands was a popular activity.

Children were also captivated by television. Shows such as *Howdy Doody* attracted a devoted audience of baby boomers.

## Bobby-soxers

Teenage girls in the 1940s who were known as bobby-soxers liked to wear striped football socks along with their baggy, rolled-up blue jeans and sloppy shirttails. For laughs, they would often purposely wear mismatched socks and shoes.

A favorite bobby-soxer hangout was the local soda shop. There they could listen to their favorite songs on the jukebox. They were passionate about dancing the lindy, a form of the jitterbug, to the big-band swing music of Glenn Miller, Count Basie, Benny Goodman, and others. But bobby-soxers went absolutely crazy over a blue-eyed young singer with a smooth voice.

Francis Albert "Frank" Sinatra caused screams and squeals of ecstasy from girls in the audience as soon as he began to croon a romantic ballad. Some bobby-soxers had to be carried away on stretchers. On October 12, 1944, Sinatra was performing at the Paramount Theater in New York City. While the concert was going on, about thirty thousand bobby-soxers were rioting outside the theater in Times Square. Hundreds of riot police officers were rushed in to calm the crowd.

## Popular Music

Big-band swing music, the danceable jazz of the 1930s, maintained its popularity during the 1940s. But later in the decade, young people were drawn to rhythm and blues, a style of music that would evolve into rock 'n' roll in the 1950s. With a few exceptions, such as the Duke Ellington Orchestra, the popularity of swing bands began to decline. Duke Ellington, one of America's great composers, had transformed his swing band into a jazz orchestra that performed his concert pieces, such as *Black, Brown, and Beige*, in places such as Carnegie Hall.

Other jazz musicians in the 1940s, such as Charlie "Bird" Parker, John Birks "Dizzy" Gillespie, Earl "Bud" Powell, and Theolonious Monk, were creating a new type of jazz that came to be called bebop. The new bebop style featured brilliant improvisation built on complex harmonic structures, played at almost impossibly fast tempos. People who wanted to dance had to go elsewhere. Bebop was for people who wanted to *listen* to music. Bebop was typically performed by small groups—trios, quartets, or quintets. Unlike swing, bebop never became music for a mass audience, but it retained an audience of devoted jazz fans for decades to come.

*Dizzie Gillespie was one of the greatest jazz trumpeters of all time.*

Jackie Robinson broke the race barrier in professional baseball.

# Sports

As with factory work, the war years opened up sporting opportunities to women. Postwar, they would also open up to African Americans. And after a decade-long absence, the Olympics made a triumphant return and did their part in trying to restore worldwide good will.

## Jackie Robinson Breaks the Color Barrier

Major-league baseball was for whites only until 1947. That was the year that Branch Rickey, the General Manager of the Brooklyn Dodgers, decided that the time had come to integrate professional baseball. He hired Jack Roosevelt "Jackie" Robinson to become the first African American to play in the major leagues.

Robinson was born in Georgia in 1919. He was a sports star in high school and college. During World War II, he served as an officer in the US Army and was dismayed by the army's rule about segregating black and white soldiers. After the war, Jackie Robinson chose to confront segregation in major league baseball by taking up Ricky on his offer.

At first, Robinson had to put up with abuse and harassment from prejudiced fans and ball players. But Robinson soon proved his worth to the team. During his first season in 1947, Robinson scored 125 runs. He managed to steal 29 bases that season, more than anyone else in the league. He was named Rookie of the Year in 1947. Robinson was mainly a second baseman, but he also played as an outfielder and as a first and third baseman. In 1949, he was named the National League's Most Valuable Player. That year, he scored 122 runs, batted in 124 runs, had a total of 203 hits, and led the league with a batting average of .342 and 37 stolen bases.

Once Jackie Robinson broke the color barrier in major league baseball, other African Americans followed in his footsteps. Before the decade was over, Don Newcombe began pitching for the Dodgers. The New York Giants signed Hank Thompson and Monte Irvin. Satchel Paige, Larry Doby, and Luke Easter joined the American League's Cleveland Indians.

## A League of Their Own

Some of the most memorable images of the war years are photographs of famous baseball players, such as New York Yankee Joe DiMaggio, enlisting to serve in the army. With so many men overseas in combat, there were not enough men left to play major league baseball.

To keep the game going so people left on the home front could enjoy America's favorite pastime, chewing gum tycoon and Chicago Cubs owner Philip Wrigley decided to try to replace the departing baseball players with women. Just as women stepped up to take factory jobs left behind by men, women of ages fifteen to twenty-five joined the All-American Girls Professional Baseball League beginning in 1943.

Although some minor points of the game were changed, such as overhand pitching, the women played just like men did—but they did it wearing short dresses with satin undergarments! The league had its peak year in 1948, when more than nine hundred thousand people came out to watch the ten women's teams play their season. By 1952,

Women's leagues satisfied baseball fans during the war.

*Figure skater Dick Button won the gold at the 1948 Winter Olympics.*

the end of the war and the return of men's baseball caused attendance to dwindle. The league closed down, but it remains memorable for the unique opportunity it gave women of the time.

## The Olympics Return

In February 1948, American Dick Button won the gold medal for men's figure skating while Sweden took first place in women's figure skating at the Winter Olympic Games, held in St. Moritz, Switzerland. In second and third place were Switzerland and the United States. But the figure skating event, or any other event, was not necessarily as interesting as the fact that the Olympic Games were taking place at all. The 1948 Olympics were the first held since 1936. The games had been suspended because of World War II, which had involved a huge number of the world's nations. So the 1948 games were especially exciting for all those involved.

## Citation Wins the Triple Crown

The racehorse Citation galloped his way to a Triple Crown victory after having won the Kentucky Derby, Preakness Stakes, and in July 1948, the Belmont Stakes. Citation was ridden by jockey Eddie Arcaro, who had been victorious with Citation before. In fact, after the 1948 Triple Crown win, Arcaro could count four Kentucky Derby wins, two Preakness Stakes wins, and four Belmont Stakes wins—all with Citation. Arcaro's prize money, a total of more than $645,000, was a record for a rider with just one horse.

# National and International Politics

President Franklin Delano Roosevelt was elected to his third term in office in 1940. In order to win the election, he had to walk a fine line between isolationists—Americans who wanted the country to stay out of the war in Europe—and interventionists—those who wanted to join the conflict.

## Avoiding War

Some interventionists believed that America had to act to bring peace and stability to Europe and Asia for the sake of trade and commerce. Some were for direct military involvement. Others thought economic measures would be enough. Roosevelt believed that military intervention would be necessary, but America was not yet ready for this step.

Among the interventionists were Jewish Americans and others who feared that Adolf Hitler, the leader of Nazi Germany, was determined to destroy Europe's Jews. Since coming to power, Hitler had passed laws taking away the rights of German Jews. Now he was taking over other nations, and he seemed ready to threaten Jews in those countries, too. Still, opposition to involvement in the war remained strong.

To strike a compromise, Roosevelt told the nation that he would not send Americans to fight overseas. Instead, America would send

Adolf Hitler spread his hateful agenda throughout Europe.

the Allies—Great Britain, France, and other nations—enough military supplies to enable them to defeat the Axis Powers—Germany, Italy, and Japan. Though technically neutral, the United States had chosen sides. And in September 1940, Roosevelt signed the Selective Training and Service Act. This law paved the way to draft men between the ages of twenty-one and thirty-five into the military.

## Choosing Sides

In his State of the Union address on January 6, 1941, Roosevelt spelled out the "four essential freedoms" for which the Allies were fighting, "freedom of speech, freedom of worship, freedom from want, and freedom from fear."

In early 1941, American and British war planners held secret discussions to coordinate a military strategy against the Axis Powers. In March 1941, Congress passed the Lend-Lease Act. This law made $7 billion in aid available for Great Britain. In September, after an American ship was attacked by a German submarine, Roosevelt ordered American ships to be armed.

In October, several skirmishes occurred between American and German ships. After an American destroyer was torpedoed near Greenland, Roosevelt said, "America has been attacked, the shooting has started." On October 30, the Germans sank the USS *Reuben James*. More than one hundred American seamen were killed in the attack. But Americans were still not ready to go to war.

## The Attack on Pearl Harbor

Throughout the late summer and fall of 1941, Japanese and American diplomats talked about ways to avoid war. The Japanese considered American and British economic involvement and military

# The Lend-Lease Act

The Lend-Lease Act allowed President Roosevelt to lend or lease US property to other nations involved in the war. It was a way of helping the Allied Forces without actually fighting in the war. Roosevelt sent everything from combat boots to cargo ships to old World War I warships. Most of the aid went to Britain and China. Later, the Soviet Union and thirty-four other countries received United States help as well.

The Lend-Lease program lasted until the end of the war. America sent roughly $50 billion in equipment to other countries. Lend-Lease was an important part of the Allied war effort. It helped stop the Axis advance.

*Japan attacked the naval base at Pearl Harbor on December 7, 1941.*

presence in Asia as a threat to their own dominance of the region. At the same time, Japanese military leaders were making plans for a possible attack on Pearl Harbor in Hawaii, where the US Navy had a large fleet of ships. Japanese war planners believed that without these ships, America would be helpless to stop Japan from expanding its empire. When differences could not be settled through diplomacy, Japan prepared to attack. This would prove to be the event that would bring America into the war.

By late November, a fleet of warships secretly set sail from Japan. There were cruisers, destroyers, battleships, and submarines. Most importantly, there were six aircraft carriers holding roughly four hundred airplanes. Even as the Japanese fleet steamed toward Hawaii for a surprise attack, Japanese diplomats continued peace talks in Washington, D.C.

On December 6, American code-breaking specialists intercepted and decoded a long message to the Japanese diplomats. The message convinced President Roosevelt and his aides that Japan was planning to attack very soon. But it was impossible to say exactly where. Another intercepted message, decoded on the morning of December 7, indicated that the attack would come that very day at 1 P.M. Washington, D.C., time. A warning was sent to commanders at Pearl Harbor, but it did not arrive in time. By 6 A.M. Honolulu time, the Japanese fleet was close enough to Hawaii to start the attack.

The first wave of airplanes took off from their carriers. They appeared over Pearl Harbor shortly before 8 a.m. The American soldiers and sailors were caught completely by surprise. Bullets, bombs, and torpedoes rained down from the sky. A Japanese bomber scored a direct hit on the USS *Arizona*. A second wave arrived soon after. The huge battleship exploded and sank, which killed most of the crew. In total, eight battleships and thirteen other naval vessels were sunk or damaged, 188 aircraft were destroyed, 2,335 United States military personnel were killed, and 1,178 were wounded. The humiliating, ninety-minute sneak attack outraged Americans and finally changed their minds about entering the war.

The following day, President Roosevelt asked Congress for a declaration of war against Japan. He described December 7, 1941, as "a date which will live in infamy." America joined the Allies, and in response, Germany and Italy declared war on the United States.

## Civilian Casualties

As the war went on, it became clear that this war differed from previous wars in one important way. In many respects, World War II was a war against civilians. The Nazis in Germany eagerly helped Hitler carry out his genocidal war against the Jews. In what has come to be called the Holocaust, Hitler succeeded in murdering six million Jews, which was half of the world's total. Almost six million others, including Gypsies and Russian prisoners of war, were also murdered in concentration camps set up by the Nazis to eliminate those they considered inferior.

Hitler also bombed cities in Great Britain and other places in Europe. During the German Army's nine-hundred-day siege of Leningrad, now St. Petersburg, in the Soviet Union, more than one third of the population of three million died of starvation. However, the German Nazis were not alone in their attacks on civilians. Seeking to force the total surrender of the Japanese military, the United States dropped atomic bombs on the cities of Hiroshima and Nagasaki. These weapons were more devastating than anything the world had seen before.

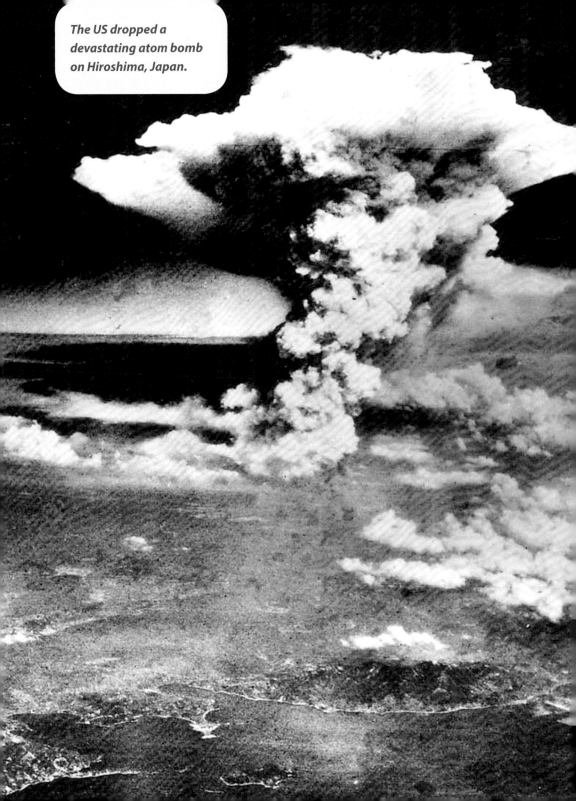

The US dropped a devastating atom bomb on Hiroshima, Japan.

Japanese Americans were forced into camps until the war was over.

# Plight of Japanese Americans

Ironically, while struggling to defeat the perpetrators of genocidal racism abroad, Americans resorted to a shameful racist policy at home. In 1942, President Roosevelt ordered the internment of more than 110,000 Japanese Americans in concentration camps, known as relocation centers, in the western deserts of the United States. The American concentration camps were not death camps like those of the Nazis, but Japanese Americans were forced to give up their homes for the duration of the war.

After the attack on Pearl Harbor, anger at Japan quickly became directed at Japanese Americans, most of whom lived in California. On the grounds that some Japanese Americans might be spies and commit acts of sabotage, Roosevelt signed Executive Order 9066. It provided for the roundup and evacuation of Japanese Americans to relocation centers. Families were forced to sell property in a hurry, and they often had to practically give it away.

When the war ended, Japanese Americans returned home to find there was no way to get back their property. As a result of their internment in relocation centers, Japanese Americans lost more than $400 million in property and income.

Even though they had been subjected to terrible treatment, most Japanese Americans remained loyal to the United States. Many were determined to show their loyalty by making American flags and saluting them each morning. Young Japanese American men even served in the armed forces. One regiment was made up of camp internees and the other of Japanese soldiers from Hawaii. The all-Japanese 442nd Regimental Combat Team became one of the most highly honored military units in American history. Four decades later, the US government admitted its mistake when President Ronald Reagan publicly apologized for the treatment of Japanese Americans during World War II.

# A. Philip Randolph and Civil Rights

Japanese Americans were not the only minority in the United States during the 1940s who were the victims of racism. African Americans had long been struggling against discrimination, and the 1940s brought some progress.

In January 1941, A. Philip Randolph, the head of the Brotherhood of Sleeping Car Porters, an all-black union, organized the March on Washington Movement (MOWM). The MOWM made plans for a huge march on Washington by African Americans. The marchers would demand an end to discrimination in defense plants and segregation in the armed forces. When President Roosevelt learned of this march, he issued Executive Order 8802. It called for an end to discrimination in government agencies, job-training programs, and by defense contractors. Randolph called off the march. Segregation continued in the military until July 1948, when President Truman ended it with an executive order.

One of the most influential labor and civil rights leaders in American history, Randolph also set up the Fair Employment Practices Committee to oversee the way Roosevelt's Executive Order 8802 was carried out.

Although millions of African Americans served in the military overseas, the armed forces were segregated throughout the war. All-black combat units served with distinction under General George Patton at the Battle of the Bulge during the winter of 1944 to 1945. Even so, African Americans, having risked their lives fighting for their country, still had a long fight ahead to win full civil rights.

# Code Talkers and Discrimination

Although Mexican Americans also suffered from discrimination in the United States, nearly 350,000 served in the armed forces. A disproportionately higher number of them, compared to other groups

A. Philip Randolph *(left) stands with Adam Clayton Powell.*

of Americans participating in the war, earned Congressional Medals of Honor and citations for distinguished service. After the war, Mexican-American veterans organized groups to fight for civil rights.

Twenty-five thousand American Indians also served in the armed forces during the war. Among them were many Navajo code talkers. They provided an essential service by relaying secret military messages in a code based on their native language that the Japanese were unable to decipher. About fifty thousand Indians left their reservations to work in defense industries. But Indians in America still faced continual discrimination. Earlier government programs aimed at preserving tribal lands and ways of life were set aside by lawmakers determined to "free Indians from the reservations" and end benefits for Indians at the taxpayers' expense. In response to this attempt to end all reservations, Indians in 1944 organized the National Congress of American Indians.

## Germany Betrays the Soviet Union

The war in Europe had started on September 1, 1939, when Hitler invaded Poland. Great Britain and France had responded by declaring war on Germany. But things did not go well for the British and French armies. In the spring of 1940, Hitler trapped the British Army in France between his forces and the sea. Between May 27 and June 4, about 340,000 British soldiers were evacuated from the beaches at Dunkirk in hundreds of small boats.

On June 17, 1940, Hitler's army occupied Paris and set up a puppet government with Vichy as its capital. Next on Hitler's agenda was an invasion of England. This proved to be a mistake. All of Hitler's air power and bombs failed to force the British to give up. So Hitler turned to a new target in the east, the Soviet Union. This, too, would prove to be a mistake.

In 1939, Joseph Stalin, the leader of the Soviet Union, had shocked the world by signing a nonaggression pact with Hitler. The two dictators agreed not to attack each other and to divide Eastern Europe between themselves.

On June 22, 1941, however, Hitler launched a massive surprise invasion of the Soviet Union. More than three million men attacked. Facing only light resistance from the Soviet Army, which was not prepared for Hitler's *blitzkrieg*, or lightning war, the Nazi invaders quickly captured much of Ukraine in the western Soviet Union.

The German Army came close to Moscow but was unable to advance any farther. The Germans were also unable to capture Leningrad, even after a nine-hundred-day siege. But it was at Stalingrad that the Nazis suffered their greatest defeat.

On January 31, 1943, after five months of brutal fighting, the Germans surrendered to the Soviets. Stalingrad had been totally destroyed. About 750,000 Russian soldiers and civilians were dead. But the Germans had lost about 200,000 men, and another 108,000 were taken prisoner. This was the first major Nazi defeat of the war. It was also the beginning of the end for Hitler.

## The Allies Welcome Stalin

American president Franklin Roosevelt and British prime minister Winston Churchill had worked out a strategy for winning the war. They would enter an alliance with Stalin even though neither trusted the Soviet dictator. Stalin, on the other hand, suspected that his new allies were only too happy to let Russia bear the worst of the Nazi aggression. In fact, the Soviet Union suffered far greater losses than any other nation. By the time the war was over, 25 million Soviets had died, compared to the 2 million British and 322,000 Americans.

After Stalingrad, the Soviet Army began its push westward to retake the lands occupied by the Nazis. In July 1943, the Soviets defeated the

Soviet troops finally defeated the Germans at the ravaged Stalingrad.

A German tank rolls to impending defeat at the Battle of Kursk.

Germans at Kursk. Meanwhile, the Allies, having defeated the German and Italian forces in North Africa, invaded Sicily on July 10, 1943. They were now prepared to invade mainland Italy. On July 25, Italian dictator Benito Mussolini was forced to resign. He was also arrested, but he escaped. Italy surrendered to the Allies on September 3, 1943.

## The Allies Liberate Europe

At first, Adolf Hitler's war machine had seemed unstoppable. Then he reached too far. Hitler's invasion of the enormous Soviet Union meant that Germany would have to fight on two huge fronts at the same time. Soviet troops attacked from the east. Meanwhile, the other Allies closed in from the west. America's entry into the war in 1941 was a fatal blow to Germany. For two years, US troops poured into Britain. They prepared to sail across the English Channel and land in Nazi-held France. Roosevelt, Churchill, and Stalin met in Teheran, Iran, in November and December 1943 to plan Operation Overlord—the D-Day invasion of France, which was still occupied by the Germans.

The D-Day invasion, under the command of General Dwight D. Eisenhower, took place on June 6, 1944. Five thousand ships carried 156,000 men across the English Channel in the largest seaborne invasion in history. When the Allied forces came ashore, they suffered heavy casualties before securing the beaches at Normandy, France. On August 25, United States troops, along with French troops under General Charles de Gaulle, entered Paris and freed the city from German rule.

In December 1944, Hitler's forces made a final assault and attacked American soldiers in Belgium and Luxembourg. The German advance captured a large area of land that looked like a big bulge on a map, so the attack came to be known as the Battle of the Bulge. However, the American troops rallied and won the ground back. The Battle of the Bulge had been Hitler's last hope. Germany would soon lose the war.

# Franklin Delano Roosevelt

Franklin D. Roosevelt guided America through some of its toughest times. First, he battled the Great Depression. Later, he inspired hope during the darkest hours of World War II. Roosevelt was a determined man, but by 1944 his health was failing. When he died in April 1945, a stunned nation mourned.

Even before he became president, FDR had health problems. Polio had robbed him of the use of his legs. Roosevelt never let the public see him in a wheelchair. When giving speeches in front of people, he usually stood upright with help from an aide.

By 1945, the stress of leading a nation during wartime was wearing on Roosevelt. In April of that year, Roosevelt was resting at a resort in Georgia. On the afternoon of April 12, he complained of a terrible headache. He died quietly a short time later. FDR had poured all of his strength into being president. Yet he did not live long enough to see the Allies' final victory in World War II.

In February 1945 at the Yalta Conference, Roosevelt, Churchill, and Stalin worked out plans for the postwar occupation of Germany. Soviet troops entered Berlin, Germany, in mid-April and fought a final victorious battle against Nazi troops. Germany surrendered to the Allies on May 8. Known as VE (Victory in Europe) day, it marked the end of World War II in Europe.

Roosevelt, who was serving his fourth term in office as president, didn't live to see the victory. He died of a stroke on April 12, 1945. His vice president, Harry Truman, took over the presidency.

The Axis leaders, too, suffered death as the war came to a close. Benito Mussolini was murdered on April 28 by Italian partisans. Adolf Hitler and his wife, Eva Braun, committed suicide on April 30 during the last days of the Battle of Berlin.

## Nazi Concentration Camps

In the spring of 1943, while his armies were being destroyed by the Soviets, Hitler seemed even more intent on murdering the last of the Jews in the Warsaw ghetto. Most of the half million Jews who had been confined to the Warsaw ghetto in 1940 had already been sent to concentration camps. Knowing they were doomed, the Jews still in the ghetto mounted an armed uprising against the Nazis in April 1943. Weeks later, in May, the battle was over. The Nazi troops had totally destroyed the ghetto and killed most of the defenders. Only a handful of Jewish fighters managed to escape by way of the Warsaw sewers.

As the Allies freed territory from Nazi rule, they discovered Hitler's concentration camps. They were horrified to learn that millions of innocent people had been tortured and killed in these places. Those who survived were starving and ill. The cruelty and suffering of the concentration camps shocked the world.

# Striking Back in the Pacific

While the war raged in Europe, Japanese forces were on the march throughout Southeast Asia and the Pacific. By July 1942, the Japanese occupied islands in the Pacific, Manchuria, eastern China, Korea, Burma, Thailand, Singapore, French Indochina, Malaya, New Guinea, and the Philippines. Many of these were British or American colonies.

The United States had suffered a humiliating blow at Pearl Harbor. But American morale began to improve when the US Navy defeated the Japanese at the Battle of the Coral Sea in May 1942. Then on June 4 through 6, US Navy pilots under the command of Admiral Chester Nimitz succeeded in destroying Japan's main naval force during the Battle of Midway.

One by one, the Pacific Islands were won from the Japanese. America won major victories at Guadalcanal in the Solomon Islands, the Bismarck Sea, the Gilbert Islands, the Marshall Islands, and the Philippine Sea.

In May 1943, US troops also defeated the Japanese at the Battle of Attu Island in Alaska's Aleutian Islands. The Japanese had invaded the islands of Attu and Kiska in June 1942. This was the only foreign occupation of US territory during World War II except for Guam. Most of the 2,600 Japanese troops on Attu died in the battle. The 6,000 Japanese troops on Kiska escaped by ship through a thick fog.

American General Douglas MacArthur recaptured the Philippines in October 1944. During the Battle of Leyte Gulf, the Japanese resorted to suicidal kamikaze attacks, crashing their planes into American ships.

In November, American pilots began a series of bombing raids on Japan. Further American victories occurred during the first half of 1945 at Iwo Jima and Okinawa. In May 1945, the Allies retook Burma.

On August 6, after Japan refused to surrender, President Truman ordered the dropping of the first atomic bomb on Hiroshima. Roughly

*Hitler's Nazis forced European Jews into concentration camps.*

US naval pilots were victorious at the Battle of Midway.

seventy thousand people died instantly. Tens of thousands of others were left severely injured, and many of them would die in the coming months. Truman warned that another bomb would be dropped if Japan did not surrender. Japanese leaders refused to do so. Three days after the attack on Hiroshima, another US bomber appeared over the city of Nagasaki. This time forty thousand people were killed instantly. Japan's leaders at last gave up. On August 14, 1945, they surrendered to the Allies. The Axis powers had been defeated, and the war was over.

## Recovery and Rebuilding

When the fighting ended and the celebrations were over, it was time to put together a world that had been smashed to bits. Survivors stumbled through destroyed cities while searching for food. Fortunately for Americans, the United States had been spared the ravages of war. So America was faced with the task of leading the recovery and rebuilding of the ruined nations, including the defeated enemies Germany, Italy, and Japan.

In June 1947, George C. Marshall, the US Secretary of State, proposed a massive economic aid package for Europe to alleviate "hunger, poverty, desperation, and chaos." The American government hoped the Marshall Plan would encourage Western European countries to install or keep democratic governments rather than becoming communists. At the same time, the United States hoped to create a market for American goods.

There also was the matter of bringing to justice those who were guilty of war crimes. The Allies held trials in Nuremberg, Germany. All the Nazi leaders brought to trial pled not guilty—they were just obeying orders. This so-called Nuremberg defense was ignored. Some Nazis were hanged. Others received lengthy prison terms.

In Japan, former Premier Hideki Tojo and six others were indicted on fifty-five counts of war crimes. The seven were condemned to hang. Tojo was executed on December 23, 1948.

## Containing Communism

Also in 1947, President Truman announced a strategy for containing communism. The plan would try to prevent communism from spreading beyond those nations where it already existed. This led to increasing friction with the Soviet Union. In April 1949, the United States and its European allies created the North Atlantic Treaty Organization (NATO), a mutual defense alliance to protect members against Soviet attack.

After the war, Germany was divided into four zones: British, French, Soviet, and American. The Soviets occupied the eastern zone. The city of Berlin was divided into French, American, British, and Soviet sectors. As relations between America and the Soviet Union deteriorated, West Berlin became a flashpoint. Because West Berlin lay within the eastern zone of Germany, the Soviets controlled access to the city. When relations became especially tense in 1948, the Soviets blocked all traffic from reaching West Berlin from the west. America and Great Britain mounted an airlift of supplies to West Berlin that lasted from June 1948 until May 1949. On May 23, 1949, during the Berlin Airlift, the British, French, and American occupation zones of Germany became the Federal Republic of Germany (West Germany). Civilian rule began there in September 1949. On October 7, 1949, the Soviet zone became the German Democratic Republic (Communist East Germany). The other countries of Eastern Europe, one by one through the postwar years, became communist satellites of the Soviet Union. An "Iron Curtain," in the words of Winston Churchill, descended across Europe, dividing the communist East from the democratic West.

HARD WHEAT FLOUR (BLENDED)
**PLAIN**
CONTRACT NO. A 1 pin (FC) 20547
NET WEIGHT 100 LBS.
GROSS WT. 100.5 LBS
COMMODITY CODE 45-85-100
MANUFACTURED BY
COMMANDER LARABEE MILLING CO.
GENERAL OFFICES
MINNEAPOLIS, MINNESOTA
MADE IN U.S.A.

*Under the Marshall Plan, the US sent food to European nations.*

Soviet soldiers fly the Red Flag over their zone in Berlin.

In Japan, meanwhile, American occupation forces under the command of General Douglas MacArthur began the process of transforming the nation into a democracy. Although Emperor Hirohito was allowed to keep his title, his role would be solely ceremonial.

## United Nations

Once before, there had been an attempt to preserve peace in the world. After World War I, the Treaty of Versailles had provided for the establishment of a League of Nations. Unfortunately, an isolationist America had refused to join the League, and it ultimately failed to keep the peace. In 1945, there could be no turning away from the goal of peace among nations. In June 1945, fifty nations, including the United States and the Soviet Union, signed the United Nations Charter. The charter pledged "to save succeeding generations from the scourge of war." The new peacekeeping organization consisted of several parts, including the General Assembly, in which each member nation could cast its vote, and the Security Council, which has eleven members. The Security Council has six rotating members and five permanent ones: the United States, the Soviet Union (now Russia), Great Britain, France, and China. Each permanent member can veto any Security Council action.

In 1946, President Truman appointed Eleanor Roosevelt, widow of the late president, as a delegate to the United Nations (UN). On December 10, 1948, the UN Commission on Human Rights approved the Universal Declaration of Human Rights, which Eleanor Roosevelt had helped write. For many years, she had worked to promote human rights and justice in the world. In the years to come, Eleanor Roosevelt would continue to be an inspiration to American women and work to make the world a better place.

# India Wins Independence

New challenges to a peaceful world seemed to be popping up all over. Great Britain, realizing it could no longer maintain its global empire, granted independence to its colony of India. On August 15, 1947, British official Lord Louis Mountbatten, the last viceroy (British ruler) of India, partitioned India into two independent countries—India and Pakistan—because of what seemed to be irreconcilable differences between Hindus and Muslims. Almost immediately, fighting broke out. The tensions also led to the death of Mohandas "Mahatma" Gandhi, the man who had led the resistance to British rule and had inspired people all over the world with his ideals of nonviolence. On January 30, 1948, Gandhi was assassinated by a Hindu fanatic who was angry at Gandhi's efforts to bring about equal treatment for all Indians regardless of their religion.

# A Jewish State

Much of the Middle East, including Palestine, had also been under the control of Great Britain. Palestine's population of Arabs greatly outnumbered its Jewish population. Palestine had once been the homeland of the Jewish people. Although the Romans had driven most of Palestine's Jews into exile eighteen hundred years earlier, a small population of Jews had always lived there. Their numbers began to increase as Jewish refugees from the Holocaust in Europe arrived. After the war, survivors of the Holocaust also came. Fighting often broke out between Jews and Arabs.

In 1947, the British gave up control of Palestine to the United Nations. The General Assembly decided to separate Palestine into a Jewish section and an Arab section. The Arabs did not accept this plan. When the Jews announced the birth of their new nation of Israel on May 14, 1948, Arab armies from Egypt, Syria, Iraq, Jordan, and

# Mahatma Gandhi

A crucial leader in India's independence from Britain, Mohandas Gandhi taught that freedom could be achieved without violence. The Indian people called him Mahatma, which means great soul. In 1858, India officially became a British colony. However, during the early 1900s, some Indians wanted to break away from Britain. Gandhi found peaceful ways to protest British rule. For example, he advised Indians not to pay their taxes and not to buy things made in Britain. The British government arrested Gandhi many times. While in jail, he often refused to eat. These fasts worried the British authorities, who knew that the Indian people would revolt if Gandhi starved to death in prison.

In 1947, Gandhi saw his dream come true when India gained its independence. A year later, a religious fanatic shot and killed him. The assassin was an Indian Hindu who was angry that Gandhi had helped Indian Muslims to create the state of Pakistan. Gandhi was seventy-eight years old when he died. The world mourned his passing. During the 1950s and beyond, Gandhi's work inspired many other peaceful movements around the globe. In the United States, Martin Luther King Jr. adopted Gandhi's methods to draw attention to the problems facing African Americans.

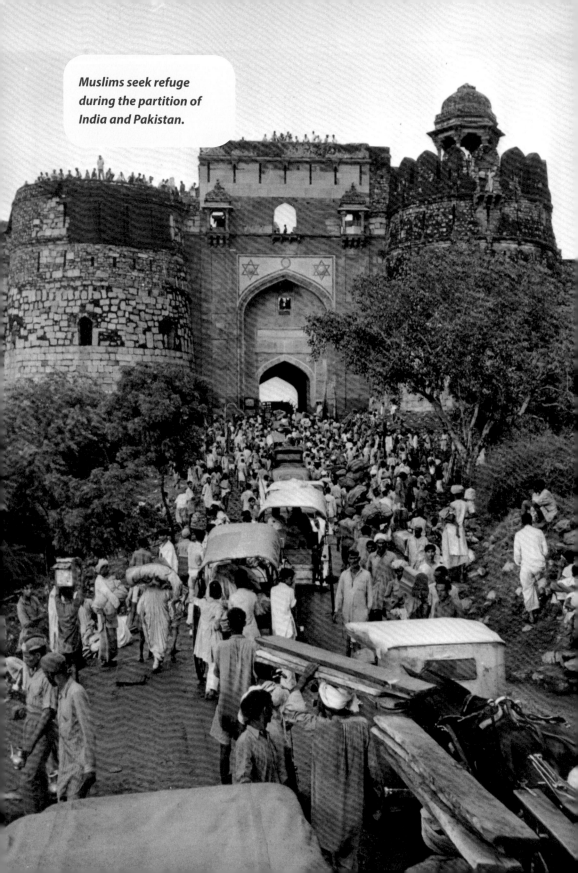

Muslims seek refuge during the partition of India and Pakistan.

**Jews assemble in the streets of Tel-Aviv to celebrate the announcement of the new Jewish state of Israel.**

Lebanon attacked within hours. Israel won its desperate struggle for survival, but seeds of bitterness were sown that would lead to more wars in the future.

## People's Republic of China

China in the late 1940s was the scene of a brutal civil war between Mao Zedong's communists and Jiang Jieshi's nationalists. The civil war had actually begun in the 1930s, but it was suspended when

Japan invaded China in 1937. Both sides then united to resist the Japanese. Once Japan surrendered in 1945, the civil war resumed. Ultimately, Mao's forces prevailed. Jiang and his supporters fled to the island of Taiwan. There they remained, claiming to be the legitimate Chinese government. By October 1949, Mao had gained control of all mainland China. He proclaimed it the People's Republic of China. Now American policymakers were faced with a huge new communist nation and the threat of a potential new enemy.

Mao Zedong proclaims China the People's Republic of China.

# Advances in Science, Technology, and Medicine

The 1940s featured the invention of two technologies that would be improved in later decades, the instant camera and the computer. More importantly, the decade saw the widespread use of medicines that saved millions, as well as the invention of the atom bomb, with its power to annihilate even more lives.

## Treating Infection and Disease

The antibiotic known as penicillin had been discovered accidentally on mold in 1928. In 1941, it was first used successfully to treat a bacterial infection. The timing of this medical development could not have been better. American army medics would soon be faced with huge numbers of wounded soldiers in need of something to stop infection. Luckily, they now had penicillin, which went into mass production in 1943. After testing several kinds of mold, scientists discovered streptomycin in 1944. In 1945, it became the first antibiotic used successfully in the treatment of tuberculosis.

The army had another reason to be grateful to scientists. United States troops fighting in the jungles of the South Pacific frequently came down with malaria, a deadly tropical illness transmitted by mosquitoes. In 1944, when scientists achieved the first total synthesis

# Germany Approaches the United States

In the early months of 1942, German U-boats, or submarines, stalked ships off America's East Coast. Submarine attacks were reported from Maine to the Carolinas. By mid-February, more than fifty cargo ships had been lost. The U-boats were most successful in North Carolina's waters, where Cape Hatteras provided an easy landmark for navigation. American sailors nicknamed the region Torpedo Junction.

At night, people on shore heard massive explosions. They saw bright orange fireballs out at sea. The next morning, debris and bodies washed ashore. The submarines were soon attacking ships in the Gulf of Mexico. They also sailed into the mouth of the Mississippi River. By June 1942, about five thousand sailors were dead, and nearly five hundred ships had been sunk. Gradually, the US Navy and Coast Guard learned to deal with the U-boat threat. When a U-boat was spotted, armed aircraft and ships rushed in to attack it. Before long, German submarine captains learned to avoid America's coastline.

A technician operates ENIAC at the University of Pennsylvania.

of quinine, they discovered that their quinine derivatives were more effective in fighting malaria than natural quinine. Soon, this new type of quinine was on its way to fight malaria in the Pacific.

## First Leap into the Computer Age

World War II was not the only event of the 1940s that would change the world. In 1946, the University of Pennsylvania created the first computer. Called ENIAC, which is short for Electronic Numerical Integrator and Computer, it could perform the functions of an ordinary calculator, but it could do so a thousand times faster than ever before. Using the flow of electrons over vacuum tubes, ENIAC was a breakthrough in science and technology. When the United States War Department made use of the computer in February 1946, it was the first organization to make the leap into what would eventually become the computer age.

## The Polaroid Camera

Perhaps not as world-changing as the first computer, another invention of the 1940s would make photography a lot more fun for many Americans. In 1948, Edwin Herbert Land introduced the Polaroid Land Camera. The camera was different because it could, in a sense, be its own darkroom because it developed film within about sixty seconds. The new Polaroid was a huge success throughout the United States.

## The Atom Bomb

The most important scientific and technological breakthrough of the 1940s, for better or worse, was the creation of the atomic bomb. Scientists were racing against time to harness the power of the atom into a weapon of mass destruction. Three physicists—Albert Einstein, who had fled to America from Nazi Germany; Enrico Fermi, who had

## Superfortress

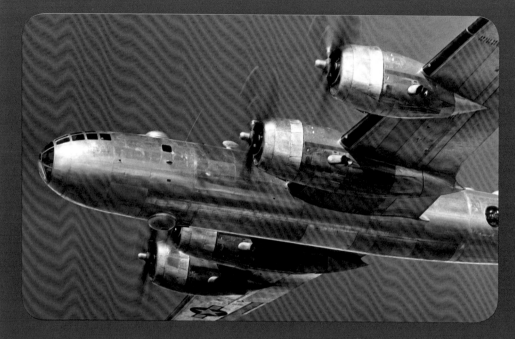

The B-29 bomber, nicknamed Superfortress, was developed for the war against Japan. The Superfortress had the longest range of any American bomber, which was about 3,000 miles (4,828 km). As American forces gained control of Pacific Islands in 1944, they built airfields. These made it possible for squadrons of B-29s to bomb Tokyo and other important Japanese cities.

fled to America from Italy; and Leo Szilard, who had sought refuge in London had written to President Franklin Roosevelt urging that the United States government try to develop nuclear weapons. It seemed certain that Adolf Hitler's scientists were attempting to do this, and it was imperative that the Allies win this race.

The Manhattan Project, which began in 1942, was the largest project in the history of science. It was directed by General Leslie

Groves of the Army Corps of Engineers. Total secrecy was imposed. Key people in the project were given code names. For example, Enrico Fermi was called Henry Farmer. Eventually, thirty-seven separate facilities employed as many as forty-three thousand people, all of them engaged in research leading to the building of the atomic bomb. However, there was so much secrecy that many of the researchers did not even know the goal of the project.

J. Robert Oppenheimer was in charge of the research complex at Los Alamos, New Mexico. It was there that the atomic bomb was built and tested. On July 16, 1945, the bomb was mounted on a steel tower and detonated. When Oppenheimer saw the giant fireball of the nuclear explosion and the mushroom cloud that rose forty thousand feet into the sky, he knew that the project had been successful. But he also wondered what horrifying implications this scientific achievement would hold for the world. "I am become death, the shatterer of worlds," were the words from a Hindu religious text that Oppenheimer recalled at that moment.

# Conclusion

World War II was the defining event of the decade of the 1940s and perhaps of the twentieth century. It was truly worldwide in scope, affecting people in every corner of the globe. But the 1940s saw more than just war. In response to the tensions in Europe, Americans looked for new ways to have fun. Hollywood produced classic films, people danced to the wild moves of the jitterbug, and singer Frank Sinatra captured the hearts of teenage girls all over the country. It was a decade of remarkable contrast and innovation.

The tragedy and turmoil of the 1940s changed the world in fundamental ways. International power shifted. Old empires collapsed, and new countries emerged. Two Allied countries that had fought together to defeat the Axis powers in World War II now began a long, bitter political struggle with each other.

At the start of the 1940s, European countries had controlled large overseas empires. But World War II had left Europe in ruins. European economies were in shambles. The European empires began to break up. In 1947, after a long campaign for independence led by Mohandas K. Gandhi, Britain gave up India, its most important colony. Two independent countries were created: India and Pakistan. France tried to hold on to its colonies but faced an exhausting war in Vietnam.

The Nazis had murdered millions of Jews during World War II. But survivors of the Holocaust and other Jews established a Jewish country, Israel. The new country was officially declared in May 1948, but Israel had to defeat its Arab neighbors in a war to survive. Though

On August 14, 1945, in Times Square, a young couple celebrate Japan's defeat.

the fighting from that war was over by the beginning of 1949, the Arab-Israeli conflict was never resolved.

In 1949, communist forces won a civil war in mainland China. On October 1, Mao Zedong declared the establishment of the People's Republic of China. A communist country, it was at first an ally of the Soviet Union.

This was not good news for the United States. America and the Soviet Union had become bitter rivals. A conflict known as the Cold War had begun. Although this struggle was very tense, the armed forces of the United States and the Soviet Union did not fight each other directly. Instead, the two superpowers tried to get other countries to support their political and economic systems and to prevent the other side from gaining allies. In Eastern Europe, the Soviet Union installed communist governments that answered to Soviet leaders. Meanwhile, the United States—under the administration of President Truman—crafted policies to prevent Western European countries from becoming communist. For example, under the Marshall Plan, the United States spent billions of dollars to rebuild Western Europe. The North Atlantic Treaty Organization (NATO) was an alliance of European countries, the United States, and Canada. It was formed in 1949 to counter the threat of communist expansion.

As the 1950s dawned, people in the United States, the Soviet Union, and all over the world worried about a direct war between the superpowers. With atomic weapons, missiles, and jets—all of which were developed during the 1940s—unimaginable destruction could come quickly and with little warning.

# Timeline

**1940**  The German Army occupies Paris, France. Germans carry out blitz bombing of London. Du Pont introduces nylon. Anti-Nazi films *The Great Dictator* and *I Married a Nazi* are released in theaters. Richard Wright's *Native Son* is published. In September, President Franklin Roosevelt signs the Selective Training and Service Act. Roosevelt wins a third term as President in November.

**1941**  On January 6, Roosevelt gives his State of the Union address. Also in January, A. Philip Randolph organizes the March on Washington Movement to fight for an end to racial discrimination. In March, Congress passes the Lend-Lease Act, which will indirectly assist the Allied war effort. In June, Hitler invades the Soviet Union. On October 30, Germans sink the USS *Reuben James*. On December 7, Japan bombs Pearl Harbor. The United States enters World War II. Penicillin is first used to treat bacterial infection.

**1942**  The US Navy defeats the Japanese at the Battle of the Coral Sea. The United States destroys Japan's main naval force at the Battle of Midway. In June, the Office of War Information is created. President Roosevelt orders the internment of more than 100,000 Japanese Americans. The film *Casablanca* is released. The Manhattan Project begins.

**1943**  On January 31, the Germans surrender to the Soviets at Stalingrad. In June, the Zoot Suit Riot takes places in Los Angeles. On July 25, Italian dictator Benito Mussolini resigns. Italy surrenders to Allies on September 3. *The North Star* is released. Orson Welles's *Citizen Kane* is released. Oklahoma! premieres. The All-American Girls Professional Baseball League begins.

**1944**  Allies' D-Day invasion of France takes place on June 6. Bobby-soxers riot outside Frank Sinatra's concert in New York City in October. American General Douglas MacArthur recaptures the Philippine Islands from Japan.

**1945**  The Yalta Conference takes place in February. Roosevelt dies on April 12. Mussolini is murdered on April 28. Hitler commits suicide on April 30. Germany surrenders to the Allies in May. Allies retake

Burma. In June, fifty nations sign the United Nations Charter. On July 16, the first atomic bomb is tested. On August 6 and 9, the United States drops atomic bombs on Hiroshima and Nagasaki, Japan. VJ day takes place on August 15. Richard Wright's *Black Boy* is published. *Carousel* premieres.

**1946** The bikini bathing suit, named for the Pacific island Bikini Atoll, is introduced. Broadway musical *Annie Get Your Gun* premieres. University of Pennsylvania introduces the first computer, ENIAC.

**1947** House Committee on Un-American Activities (HUAC) is established. In June, George Marshall unveils the Marshall Plan to rebuild Europe. In August, Great Britain partitions India and grants the former colony independence. In October, HUAC holds the Hollywood Ten hearings. Tennessee Williams's *A Streetcar Named Desire* is introduced. Jackie Robinson becomes the first African American major league baseball player.

**1948** On January 30, Mohandas Gandhi is assassinated. Norman Mailer's *The Naked and the Dead* is published. *Kiss Me, Kate* premieres. The first Olympic Games since 1936 take place. On May 14, the new nation of Israel is established. In June, the

Berlin Airlift begins. In July, jockey Eddie Arcaro and racehorse Citation win the Triple Crown. On December 10, the United Nations approves the Universal Declaration of Human Rights. Edwin Herbert Land introduces the Polaroid Land Camera.

**1949**  Arthur Miller's *Death of a Salesman* is introduced. Jackie Robinson is named the National League's Most Valuable Player. On May 23, West Germany becomes the Federal Republic of Germany. On October 7, East Germany becomes the German Democratic Republic. Mao Zedong establishes the communist People's Republic of China.

# Glossary

**aggression**—An unprovoked invasion or other hostile act.

**atomic bomb**—A very powerful weapon that releases nuclear energy.

**blacklist**—To suspect, avoid, or ban a person.

**blitzkrieg**—Meaning "lightning war" in German, it is a swift attack by troops, tanks, and planes.

**bomber**—An airplane built to carry and drop bombs.

**civilian**—A person who is not a member of the armed forces.

**concentration camp**—A Nazi-run prison where Jews, Gypsies, and other people considered undesirable were tortured and executed.

**dictator**—A ruler who has often obtained his or her position by force and has absolute power over a country.

**diplomat**—A government official who carries out negotiations with representatives of other countries.

**exports**—Goods traded or sold to another country.

**Holocaust**—The large-scale murder of European Jews and others by the Nazis.

**infamy**—Known for something shameful or horrible.

**kamikaze**—Meaning "divine wind" in Japanese, it refers to pilots who carried out suicide attacks on US ships.

**polio**—Short for poliomyelitis, a highly contagious disease that at its worst can lead to paralysis and even death.

**ration**—A fixed portion of goods or supplies.

**segregation**—The practice of keeping people separate based on race or other differences.

**torpedo**—A self-propelled underwater bomb launched by a submarine, ship, or airplane.

# Further Reading

## Books

Darman, Peter (ed.). *World War II Begins*. New York: Rosen Classroom, 2012.

Doeden, Matt. *Darkness Everywhere: The Assassination of Mohandas Gandhi* Minneapolis, Minn.: Lerner Publishing Group, 2013.

Engdahl, Sylvia. *The Atomic Bombings of Hiroshima and Nagasaki*. Detroit, Mich.: Greenhaven Press, 2011.

Frank, Anne. *The Diary of a Young Girl*. New York: Doubleday & Company, 1952.

Goldsmith, Connie. *Bombs over Bikini*. Minneapolis, Minn.: 21st Century, 2014.

Pederson, Charles E. *Jackie Robinson*. Edina, Minn.: Abdo Publishing Company, 2009.

Woog, Adam. *Pearl Harbor*. San Diego, Calif.: Referencepoint Press, 2012.

## Web Sites

**whitehouse.gov/history/presidents/fr32.html**
    Franklin D. Roosevelt's official presidential fact page.

**whitehouse.gov/history/presidents/ht33.html**
    Harry S. Truman's official presidential fact page.

**historylearningsite.co.uk/Nazi%20Germany.htm**

A wealth of information about the Nazi party.

**holocaust-history.org/**

The Holocaust History Project has documents, recordings, and other resources about the Holocaust.

**nationalww2museum.org/**

The Web site for the National World War II Museum.

# Movies

*Band of Brothers (Miniseries).* Directed by Tom Hanks et. al. New York: HBO, 2001.

A dramatazation of one company's experience in World War II.

*Flags of Our Fathers.* Directed by Clint Eastwood. Burbank, Calif.: Malpaso Productions, 2006.

The story of the Battle of Iwo Jima told from an American perspective.

# Index

Great Depression, 7, 62
Groves, Leslie, 82, 83
Guam, 64

## H

Hirohito, 71
Hiroshima, Japan, 50, 64
Hitler, Adolf, 8, 25, 44, 50, 57, 58, 61,
  63, 82
Hollywood, 25, 27, 28
Hollywood Ten, 28
Holocaust, 32, 50, 72, 84
House Committee on Un-American
  Activities (HUAC), 27, 28
*Howdy Doody*, 35

## I

India, 72, 73, 84
interventionists, 44
isolationism, 7, 44, 71
Israel, 72, 75, 84
Iwo Jima, 64

## J

Japanese-American internment, 53
Jewish people, 44, 64, 72, 84
Jieshi, Jiang, 75

## L

Land, Edwin Herbert, 81
League of Nations, 71
Lend-Lease Act, 46, 47

## M

MacArthur, Douglas, 64, 71
Mailer, Norman, 30
*Maltese Falcon, The,* 28

Manhattan Project, 82
March on Washington Movement
  (MOWM), 54
Marshall, George C., 67
Marshall Plan, 67, 86
Miller, Arthur, 30, 33
Mountbatten, Louis, 72
movies, 25, 28
Mussolini, Benito, 61, 63

## N

Nagasaki, Japan, 50, 67
*Naked and the Dead, The,* 30
National Congress of American
  Indians, 57
*Native Son,* 30
Nazis, 8, 25, 32, 44, 50, 53, 58, 61, 63,
  67, 84
Nimitz, Chester, 64
Normandy, France, 61
North Atlantic Treaty Organization
  (NATO), 68, 86
*North Star, The,* 27, 28
Nuremberg Trials, 67
nylon, 15

## O

Office of Price Administration (OPA),
  9
Office of War Information (OWI), 19,
  25, 27
Okinawa, 64
Olympic Games, 39, 43
Oppenheimer, J. Robert, 83

## P

Paige, Satchel, 40
Pakistan, 72, 73, 84
Palestine, 72

Paris, France, 15, 57, 61
Patton, George, 54
Pearl Harbor, Hawaii, 7, 25, 46, 49, 53, 64
penicillin, 78
Polaroid Land Camera, 81

## R

Randolph, A. Philip, 54
rationing, 9, 11, 15
Robinson, Jackie, 39, 40
Rockwell, Norman, 22
Roosevelt, Eleanor, 71
Roosevelt, Franklin Delano, 7, 19, 44, 46, 47, 49, 50, 53, 54, 58, 61, 62, 63, 82
Rosie the Riveter, 11, 12. *See also* women workers.

## S

Selective Service and Training Act, 46
Sinatra, Frank, 24, 35, 84
Soviet Union, 8, 27, 47, 50, 57, 61, 63, 68, 71, 86
Spock, Dr. Benjamin, 19
Stalin, Joseph, 57, 58, 61, 63
Szilard, Leo, 82

## T

television, 20, 33, 35
*Texaco Star Theater,* 33
Tojo, Hideki, 68
Treaty of Versailles, 71
Truman, Harry, 27, 54, 63, 64, 67, 68, 71, 86

## U

United Nations, 71, 72

Universal Declaration of Human Rights, 71
USS *Reuben James,* 46
USS *Arizona,* 49

## V

VE Day, 63
Vichy, France, 57
victory gardens, 11

## W

Warsaw ghetto uprising, 63
Welles, Orson, 30
Williams, Tennessee, 30, 33
Women Accepted for Volunteer Emergency Service (WAVES), 12
Women's Army Auxiliary Corps (WACs), 12
Women's Auxiliary Ferrying Squadron (WAFS), 12
women workers, 8, 11, 12, 15
World War I, 47, 71
World War II, 7, 8, 9, 19, 22, 25, 27, 28, 32, 33, 39, 43, 50, 53, 62, 63, 64, 81, 84
Wright, Richard, 30

## Y

Yalta Conference, 63

## Z

Zedong, Mao, 75, 86
zoot suit, 17

# DATE DUE

| | | | |
|---|---|---|---|
| | | | |
| | | | |
| | | | |
| | | | |
| | | | |
| | | | |
| | | | |
| | | | |
| | | | |
| | | | |
| | | | |
| | | | |
| | | | |
| | | | |
| | | | PRINTED IN U.S.A. |